My Lean Business Coach

The Blogs – Volume 1

August 2016

First Edition

ISBN: **978-1536970418**

Copyright © 2016 Jason Tisbury

All rights reserved. No part of this publication may be reproduced or transmitted in any form or by any means, electronic or mechanical, including photocopying, recording, or by any information storage and retrieval system, without the written permission of the author, except where permitted by law.

Also by Jason Tisbury:

7 Steps To A Lean Business

Pocket Happiness

Your 60 Minute Lean Business

- 5S
- Total Productive Maintenance
- Kaizen Mindset
- Standarised Work
- Just in Time
- Jidoka

Compilations:

Your 60 Minute Lean Business

- Volume 1 The Foundations
- Volume 2 The Pillars
- The Collection

Contents

Introduction 7

Accountability in the workplace 9

FIFO in the real world 11

Effective performance measurement 14

Skills analysis and resource planning 16

Do you have a lean strategy? 18

Top level support 20

Thinking about investing in technology? First things first! 22

The lean Government 24

Lean in Government – why so difficult? 27

Lean in Government – can it work? 29

The customer experience 31

Red tape 33

Culture and systems 34

A day on the gemba 36

How to solve any problem 38

Bringing back the simplicity 40

The nit picker 42

Less with more	44
Technology in your business	46
The value of the value stream map	49
Communication	51
What is in your control?	53
The epiphany	55
Collaboration	57
Your one thing	59
Lean success	61
The three pillars of business success	63
Productivity or efficiency?	65
Two out of three	67
Perfectionism or procrastination?	70
It's the results that matter	72
Supplier relationships	74
Are you a hider or a seeker?	76
Meetings; destructive or constructive	78
A great place to work!	80

The place of realism in problem solving 82

The comfort zone 84

One out all out 86

Sometimes you just don't win 88

Clear strategy 90

Tenacity 92

Customer issues 94

Where do I start? 96

Why, why, why 98

KPI's that matter 100

What is your value stream? 102

When to say 'enough is enough" 105

Process management 107

What's in a plan? 109

The real cost of inventory 113

Change management 117

When doing nothing is doing a whole lot 120

My most common 3 answers 122

The good old to do list 124

Over-Delegation 126

Customer service 128

Before root cause 130

The 5S System 132

Know when to strike 135

The seven wastes 139

What went wrong? 140

Does the name really matter? 142

The importance of contingencies 144

Effectiveness 146

Player or Spectator? 148

Introduction

Welcome to the first volume of the My Lean Business Coach blogs. I post a blog on my website www.mlbc.com.au most weeks; I discuss mostly the application of lean systems, however often digress based on my current thoughts or what is topical in business at the time.

The following posts are from 2014 and 2015 and are, for the most part, in the sequence of writing or posting. Some editing to correct grammar or spelling has been applied. Having read back through my own blog posts in compiling this book has been interesting; seeing where my thoughts were at different times over the past couple of years. You may find I have discussed the same topic more than once and you may find my thoughts are sometimes at small odds from earlier; however I think for the most part my thoughts are pretty consistent (which I must say, is a relief).

Some things written in these blogs, you won't agree with, and that's fine. We can't all agree all the time. If you find something you feel passionate about and want or need to discuss, feel free to email me at jason@mlbc.com.au or even reply to the blog on my website.

Why did I put this compilation together? Obviously for the betterment of all mankind! Seriously though, I was writing a new blog post a while back and started reading through some of my old posts. I thought to myself, "there's some good stuff here", so decided to start really reading and reviewing my thoughts from times gone; this resulted in 140 pages so I thought, "what the heck, why not share it?" I hope you enjoy the read and get something out of what is in these pages.

Accountability in the workplace

One of the most frequent complaints I hear is the lack of accountability throughout organisations. Often, these complaints come from the lower management and below on the organisation chart. Having a low level of accountability in a business creates broad problems and can stifle productivity, innovation and improvement. In essence the organisation cannot operate effectively whilst this problem exists. It's not only those directly involved with the action who suffer though, operations upstream, downstream and even in parallel streams suffer.

So why is accountability so difficult to get right? There are a number of reasons; a couple of the main ones are:

1) Poor performance monitoring.
To be accountable there must be an action or task to be held accountable to. Too often I see these actions constructed in a way which makes them difficult to measure progress or performance effectively. Just as often, I see a good action setup with poor measures or indicators attached. Both of these are caused by ineffective planning.

More frustrating, and thankfully less frequent, I see good planning in place without effective use of the measured data. The quote "What gets measured, gets managed" (Peter Drucker) is one of my favourite quotes, and it's almost perfect. Unfortunately I've noticed people using this quote to say "it's getting measured, so it must be managed" NO! It's not automatic! The data must be used in the management process.

2) Poor management and leadership.

I won't go into the management vs leadership discussion here but I will point out that there are too many managers lacking effective people management skills. Challenging your staff, holding them accountable is a positive management task. If this is practiced consistently without exception your team and those around yours will be higher performing, more efficient, more effective and will have a higher morale.

Simple rule to accountability: Be consistent and don't overcomplicate it.

FIFO in the real world

First in, first out simply is a term used to describe a system of using the oldest raw materials before using newer raw materials. This is useful and important for a couple of reasons:

Raw material traceability is the major reason; by controlling what raw materials we use and when we use them we can control the life of that raw material throughout its lifecycle. This is important in most manufacturing organisations and is critical in many. In the event of a recall from the raw material supplier we can recall a smaller quantity of our output if we have good FIFO controls in place. Without these controls we would have to recall a far greater sample of our outputs which will damage not only our financial position but also and more detrimentally it will damage our brand and reputation.

Secondly, many raw materials have a shelf life; with FIFO control we can reduce our wastage, and improve the quality of our outputs by always using the freshest of inputs. This will provide more consistent processes; even for long shelf life raw materials there can often be some deterioration without "going off" this deterioration will have an impact on your process control.

So how do we use FIFO? I've seen many different systems used for FIFO, from the very basic to extremes of complexity. Some organisations use software applications for batch control, others rely on their kanban system for stock control. From my experiences there is no real "best method", but there is best practice (best practice is proven by process measurement). Many of the high performing organisations in FIFO are relying on more simple systems for their FIFO control; simple lanes, card systems, even warehouse matrices over technology. While it is true, software can provide more consistent accuracy, it is very dependent on data entry being accurate and is often removed or away from the place of storage. A simple live system at the place of use and/or storage is the way to go.

Yesterday, I had to go to the doctor; I made an appointment by phone, went to counter and registered on their system, and sat in the waiting room. There were about 5 doctors on duty and about 12 customers in the waiting room. Rather than each free doctor taking the next file in line, the doctors were allocated patients as they registered (some were seeing certain doctors others were not). One doctor while I was waiting saw 5 patients (many of these had appointment times after mine), the doctor who I was queued with saw only 2 before me. Some patients were waiting longer than others. Bad FIFO

Today I had to have a blood test at the pathology next door. They don't take appointments so I walked up to the desk to register but the desk was unattended. Instead there was a simple numbered ticket. I took ticket number 5 and sat down to wait. There were 2 pathologists on duty and 5 of us sitting in the waiting room. Each number was called in turn and the patients seen in the order they arrived. As there were 2 pathologists on duty they serviced the patients in quick time and each patient waited about the same time; if one patient took longer the next pathologist would see the next in line. Good FIFO

Now, I realise in a doctor's office there can be emergencies that take precedence and extend the waiting times; and some patients need to see certain doctors, however by assigning the cases early they are inadvertently extending the average waiting time and creating a bottle neck.

Effective performance measurement

Effective performance measurement is not difficult; what is difficult is creating a positive measurement and reporting culture in an organisation. The culture can be moulded with the right systems in place. So what are the steps to creating an effective performance measurement and reporting system?

Step 1. Define what it is you do

What exactly is the purpose of your department / organisation? What are the inputs, processes, outputs and importantly what are the outcomes. What drives you, what objectives are you aligned to? Are you customer focused or are you internally (financially) focused? Be honest about why you exist. By defining why you exist or what your purpose is you can understand what to measure.

Step 2. Understand what you need to measure. These are your KPI's

This sounds simple! Too many organisations get this wrong though. You need to define the few things, that when done right will assure success. No more than five and no less than three – they should measure:

1) Effectiveness – Does the outcome match the objective?

2) Quality – Does the output meet the specifications / customer requirements?
3) Efficiency – Was the process completed on schedule and within budget?

This will give you a balanced view of your performance both technical (output) and effectiveness (outcome). It's is important that those accountable for the measure can influence the results. It's no good holding someone accountable for the output of a production cell when the operators do not report to them as they have limited influence over the result.

Step 3. Spread the word

If you're expecting others in the department or organisation to report on their performance it's important they understand why they are reporting. Tell everyone what happens to the data, how it assists with decision making. In essence you are engaging your team so they understand where they fit into the bigger picture.

Follow these simple steps and you can have an effective performance measurement system. Remember what Peter Drucker said "What gets measured, gets managed".

Skills analysis and resource planning

Do you know if your team has the right skills to do the job?

The only way to answer this question is to first understand what skills are required. Regardless of what industry you are in, you need to deliver certain outputs, to deliver these you need to skills. The first step is to clearly define what these skills are. This information should be a part of the Position Description, however as I have seen all too often, this is a common gap!

The best way to understand what skills are required is to detail the process undertaken to deliver the outputs. From there you can define the skills required for these processes. Once you have these skills identified you can list them all and begin developing a skills matrix.

Without knowing what skills you require you cannot identify what gaps you may have across your team. Without knowing your gaps, how can you be confident of success? Management is all about empowering your team to be high performing, if you haven't analysed the skill set within the team, you are holding the team back. How can you determine if you can take on extra work if you don't know if the skills are available? How can you assure the outputs are of the expected quality if you don't understand your teams' skills? The answer to both of these questions is you can't!

Taking this further to resource planning; to be successful you have to plan. This goes for operational teams as well as strategic; if you have to deliver any project or product you have to plan the resources to be used within the processes. The greater the size of the delivery and the greater the complexity, the better the planning needs to be. Without understanding the required skills or the skills of your team you cannot plan effectively.

So the next thing you need to do with your team is define your required skills, analyse your teams skills set and identify the gaps. Without going through this process you just won't know where you are.

Do you have a lean strategy?

What is a lean strategy and why should you have one? I was thinking about this recently when someone made a comment about why their business was pulling in different directions. They have pockets of the business doing some really good initiatives, however they seem to be pulling in different directions rather than working for a common goal. This is quite a common problem.

The best of intentions and even the best of actions will deliver no more than isolated short lived improvements unless they are aligned to a greater strategy. By developing a lean business strategy you will realise longer term success that is easily built upon for even more success.

A lean strategy should sit below an organisation strategy or plan. The org plan is used to guide your business in its long term development and will include your vision, mission and values. The lean strategy is a key component and provides a roadmap for identifying and eliminating the waste in your systems and processes. Remember, waste is anything your customers are not happy to pay for.

Your lean business strategy will increase your customer base, improve your profitability, improve your customer satisfaction and improve employee morale. One of the main reasons lean sometimes gets a bad name among employees is due to a lack of strategy. When all initiatives are focussed toward achieving a common goal, employees can see how the changes will make a positive difference and are more likely to come along for the journey rather than hold back.

So is it time you start your real journey and develop your lean business strategy?

Top level support

An often asked question is "How do I get the support I need from the top level?"

Like everything else, there is a process to achieve this. Firstly, let's define what support is. When given the choice of making an improvement most top level managers would jump at the chance, as long as it is a real improvement and solves a problem. When it comes to running an improvement program or instilling an improvement culture and dedicated resources, a different level of support is required. What is needed is a visible drive and ownership by the top level management; many times this is provided in the form of an email to stakeholders and a few words spoken at the Town Hall meeting – this is not good enough.

What is required is continuous discussion and communication of the importance of every team member being a part of the improvement process. Every position in the organisation has a role to play in the improvement journey and this should be reflected in the position descriptions. Running an improvement program (Lean, Six Sigma, Business Excellence – whatever the name, the desired outcomes are similar) goes much further than buying in a resource and running a few programs. To be successful, an organisation must change its culture; this is the difference between the successful lean businesses and the rest – culture. But how is a culture changed? Only through consistent behaviours and communication can a culture be changed. An email and some posters will do little (and may actually have an opposite effect) in creating a continuous improvement mindset in the organisation. And that is really what we are chasing, every employee, every day challenging the status quo to make small, effective improvements that in the long term compound into a better organisation.

This is driven from the top at the successful organisations because they get it. They've seen, touched and lived lean in their careers. You need to instil a belief in the top level management for them to truly believe!

Thinking about investing in technology? First things first!

51% of small business owners want to improve their systems and processes as a priority in 2013 according to research by MYOB. This number is just as high in larger corporations! The problem is many organisations leap straight into an IT solution to solve their problems. There is a better way.

By inserting an IT system over your current business processes you are missing out on a grand opportunity to work on your business and will be embedding poor work practices into the system.

Take the opportunity to review your business processes before implementation of a system; actually, review them before you buy! I often see businesses with fantastic IT systems purchased and installed that just don't meet their needs! This is an extremely common problem unfortunately, meaning the business has wasted money and time but is no better off; often they are worse off.

Spend some time challenging the processes involved, the time spent is well worth it.

- Map out the current state
    - Include documentation, workflow, databases etc.
- Challenge every step
    - What works well?

- Where is the waste?
- Are there any challenges or struggles?
- Brainstorm alternatives and countermeasures
- Develop an action plan and begin implementing and testing the changes
    - Remember PDCA!
- When the process is working smoothly (and is robust) without technology, find an IT solution that best meets your needs.

Now you can be sure your money will be well spent (or you may identify you don't even need to spend it after all!).

The lean Government

This is my challenge to all governments, at all levels of government. Lean management really is a perfect fit for government!

We all know about the benefits of lean management when applied effectively in the private sector, well the benefits are greater and have far greater impact when lean management is effectively applied in government. Let's take a look at some of the benefits:

- Increased efficiencies through elimination of wastes in processes.

- In the private sector this results in a corresponding reduction in costs associated with the process which can result in increased profits when effectively managed.

- Think about all of the government services that are under delivered. By eliminating the wastes from the processes used to deliver these services, the same resources can be utilised to either improve the current standards of service delivery or potentially deliver more services. Now that's what I call a benefit! Not just to a few but to the entire community!

- Improved safety and quality

- In the private sector, improved safety results in happier, safer and healthier employees while improved quality results in a better outcome or product for the customers. Both improvements also result in increased profitability for the organisation.

- Improving safety and quality in government departments will also result in happier, safer and healthier employees which equates to stability. This will result in improved efficiency again! Improved quality will result in a happier community and once again, increased efficiencies! The cycle is never ending; when we do things right first time, we can move onto another activity; when we don't get it right first time we have to return and perform rework, this is waste and annoys the community.

These are just a couple of the benefits of introducing lean management to government, there are many more and they all result in the same benefits; increased efficiency, happier employees and happier communities. There is no downside when managed effectively.

So how do we get to this future state? It really is simple, but it won't be easy! We need to do two things simultaneously.

1) Bring in private sector expertise. Don't skimp, bring in the best there is to infiltrate the system and challenge the thinking.

2) Leadership must evolve. Current leadership in many government departments is lacking lean exposure and is largely built of long term government employees. This is not

necessarily a bad thing in moderation, however when not challenged by new thinking it results in group think.

These first two steps are critical to the success of lean in government. I apologise to all of the consultants out there, however we must bring the expertise in house. Consultants have their place to bring in specialist advice, training and delivery, however without the expertise in house we will not deliver sustainable, effective lean management. Look around the world at the high performing organisations; they all have the expertise in house. Lean thinking must become a normal part of business – "the way we do things around here".

The next big change required is the structure of the departments. We need to start looking at the services as value streams and structure the business units around the delivery of services rather than the departmental, hierarchical structures currently in place. This will result in the elimination of silos that currently exist.

All of this will have its challenges, but it isn't difficult. What are you doing in your government department to make the change?

Lean in Government – why so difficult?

Having spent some time implementing Lean Systems in the government sector it is apparent that there is a perception within government that the value of a system, report, method etc. is dependent on a) the cost and B) the difficulty. If a system has a high capital cost and is difficult to implement then it must be more effective and valuable than a low cost and easily implemented system.

This is very much a misconception that must be broken if lean thinking is ever going to be highly effective in the government sector. Look at the world's greatest exponents of lean and you will see a common trait of their systems. The world leaders ensure their systems are easily accessible and easy to understand to enable the systems to be utilised by every employee within the organisation. They don't rely on big budgets to bring in expensive external consultants to evaluate or review their processes only to offer expensive fixes. The staff think lean as part of their everyday work; this creates an environment of continuous improvement.

The essence of lean is to eliminate or reduce waste from the processes and systems from the value stream. For this to be effective it is critical that this mindset be shared throughout the organisation; from the very top to the very bottom. Bringing in external facilitators at high expense to is not lean. Training employees and teams on the lean philosophy and tools and making lean a part of every employees daily working life is what lean is about. Only when this change happens at the top will lean start to become effective.

So how can this happen? Easily, the solution is to implement lean thinking from the top. When government management teams go beyond seeing lean as an opportunity to reduce costs and see it for the waste elimination system that it is the change will occur.

Lean in Government – can it work?

What makes it so difficult to implement a lean system in a Government department?

Whether you call it Lean, Six Sigma, Continuous Improvement, Business Excellence or Best Value we really are talking about the same outcome. A robust system focussing on delivering consistent value driven outcomes to the customer – in the case of a Government department the customer is the community at large in some cases and individual community members in other instances.

Just about every tool used in any other manufacturing or service organisation will work just as well in a Government department, I have found the biggest factor to address is the long standing mindset of being a Government employee. Unfortunately, many employees (across all levels of the organisations) have lost sight of why they are there. They have lost sight of the customers and the need to deliver value.

What can we do about it? Well we need to address two problems.

1) Who is the customer? Develop a customer profile with the team you are working with. Who is the customer? What do they want from your service? Go further and ask customers what they like and don't like about the service.

2) How much does the service cost and what would a similar service cost from the private sector? Now there are some Government departments who's service cannot be benchmarked against private sector, however all departments can and should be measured.

With these questions answered, you can now develop how your service should look (future state), perform a gap analysis, create an action plan and finally implement the changes.

There are two outcomes you need to achieve through this process.

1) A culture shift in the employees
2) Provide a better value and quality service to the customers

The customer experience

As most families do, we enjoy going out for a meal on the birthday of a family member, friend or other occasions. We have been going to the same few places for a couple of years now and haven't had too many complaints. Occasionally the service has been poor or the food not quite right but on the whole we have been reasonably happy customers for a couple of years.

We decided to go somewhere different for my wife's birthday recently. I have to be honest, I was a little apprehensive going away from what I knew and trusted to try something new but on the recommendation of a few friends we took the plunge.

On arrival we were greeted at the concierge desk by a friendly happy gentleman who took us to our table and made us feel right at home. We had quite a large group joining us and as each small group arrived the same smiling face brought them over to join us. We ordered our meals and bought drinks.

Now anyone with children will understand the frustration of having to wait a long time for meals with a table of 10 children waiting eagerly if not patiently. Well, to our great surprise the meals were delivered very quickly by a small army of wait staff. The food was cooked to perfection with the large variety of meals from salads to steaks delivered almost at once and the correct temperature.

After our meals we enjoyed more drinks and deserts and relaxed for the evening.

Now, I mentioned at the start of this blog that we were not unhappy with our usual places but now we have a new favourite due to their superior customer experience. I'm not sure if they even know what they did right or what they are providing but they did it.

If your customers get the opportunity to try someone else how will your customer experience bring them back?

Red tape

Good old red tape; every business has to deal with some sort of red tape. This is often imposed by regulatory bodies, customers and internally by businesses themselves for a good reason. The red tape can be a challenge for any business to cope with, however for a government department it can be suffocating as they are often under stricter scrutiny from fellow government departments. In fact the Australian Federal Government has a target to reduce the impacts of red tape by $1,000,000,000 per year. Unfortunately this is looking like actually adding some red tape due to the approach taken at least in the short term.

In every business we need some amount of red tape to ensure and monitor good corporate governance. It can become so hard to get things done that people just don't bother trying.

So how do we deal with red tape and avoid the suffocation? With good effective planning. The first step is to determine all of the regulatory and other reporting/red tape requirements.

When you have compiled a complete list of requirements the next step is to plan how you can maintain adherence to the requirements. You should add the resource requirements to your business planning process.

Through monitoring you can be sure you are fulfilling your obligations, both internal and external.

Culture and systems

What is most important, Systems or Culture? Sounds like an easy one...

Let's look at the role systems and processes play in an organisation. What are they for? Well a business has processes in place to achieve consistent, reliable outcomes and outputs. When the procedures are followed the business and customers know what they are going to get, every time. Of course this is within upper and lower tolerances and set standards.

So what role does culture play? Without the right culture in place you will have the wrong culture. There isn't any middle ground. It's either good or bad, right or wrong. Even with the most structured and robust procedures in place, if you have a bad culture (and I'm talking bad, as in people intentionally doing the wrong thing) you will not achieve consistent outcomes. It's easy to write procedures (can be time consuming), but to embed the processes and the habit takes time and culture change.

How can you tell if you have a bad culture? A bad culture can be good for another business and vice versa (within reason), so it isn't always easy to see when looking from the inside but there are always tell-tale signs. Inconsistent KPI's between departments, silo mentalities, politicking are a few signs. I believe one of the biggest causes of a bad culture is competing KPI's and lack of accountability. Often, this lack of accountability is not consistent and we will see some parts of the business being held to high account and others seemingly "untouchable". Consistently applying this is important to achieve a good, positive culture. Competing KPI's result in teams passing on a problem just to meet their individual targets. KPI's need to be cross functional to break down the silo's and bring teams together to work towards a common goal.

A day on the gemba

This week I had the opportunity to spend a whole day on the gemba, walking, observing the processes and talking to some great people. I try and spend some time on the gemba every day but unfortunately the amount of time can be too short too often. As we make our way up the ladder in any business we can find ourselves "too busy" to practice genchi gembutsu and this is a real shame for the business and more so for ourselves. We miss out on such a good learning opportunity.

So what did I learn on my day? As a manager we quite often lose sight of how the little things make a big impact on the real operations of the business. No matter what business you're in, you have activities that really count, add value to your customers and bring results to your business. If you're in a manufacturing business, this is the adding value to your raw materials to meet a customer requirement; most other activities undertaken by parts of the business are support and incidental to achieving your outcomes. The same applies if you're in the service industry; only the "face to face" or contact time matters.

The biggest thing I noticed when on my gemba walk is the amount of non-value adding time our / your value add employees spend; this could be walking, moving product, looking for something, finding information. The list is long, but it's important to remember that every minute your value adding employees are not adding value, you are losing money and your customer won't pay for whatever it is they are doing. A business is structured with value adding and incidental teams for a reason, it is your role as a manager to ensure each team is working towards delivering the expected outputs.

My other learning has been we too often forget to celebrate the small wins and achievements that occur in a business every day. It is these small wins that accumulate into the milestone achievements of a business. We must recognize our teams and their achievements regularly to develop a culture of success. Conversely, small errors, issues and failures to follow process can add up to take us further away from our goals and objectives, our customers and ultimately our success.

To succeed in business is really a simple equation: deliver on customer needs, look after your staff, be a good corporate citizen, manage your costs.

How to solve any problem

Problem solving is a powerful business tool that is often left to others to get done in businesses. Every team and every team member should be encouraged to actively participate in problem solving and the more frequently you do it the better you'll get. Here is a simple problem solving process that anyone can follow to break down any problem and develop lasting improvements.

Step 1

Define the problem

Undoubtedly the most important step in the process. If we can't define the problem, simply, we cannot provide a solution.

Step 2

Background

Is there any background information relating to the problem? How long has the problem been known? What has been attempted to fix the problem so far?

Step 3

Current state data

Data is king! This step will help take out any emotion from the problem and determine what really is a problem and what is noise.

What, when, where, frequency etc.

Pareto

Step 4

Root cause analysis

5 whys

Ishikawa

Get past the symptoms and to the real cause

Step 5

Countermeasures and corrective actions to control the root cause/s

Step 6

Action plan if required

Step 7

Evidence of resolution

Bringing back the simplicity

I've been reading a lot lately on blogs and other posts from some consultants talking about how business solutions need to be complex and the simple solutions will not work. This is total garbage. These consultants who promote this ideal are doing so to keep themselves in a job with their customers.

As business coaches, consultants etc. it should be our objective to be redundant from our clientele. We should not expect or want a long term consulting gig; our role should be to help the business management learn how to help themselves. We are there to support, not to do; by doing we are crippling the business's we are supposed to be helping.

Yes it is true that in some ways business problems have become more complex, but that is largely the doing of the consultants themselves. The size of the problems are bigger and broader but the problems and challenge themselves are really the same as 20 years ago, they're the same as 50 years ago. We need to bring back simple!

I'm not saying the answer to every problem is simple or should be, but conversely the answer to every problem does not have to be complex. The best approach is to find the most simple solution you can for each problem. For any problem to be solved there are a number of approaches one can take, ranging in complexity, that provide sufficient control while also providing a workable solution. Notice the word "workable"; what we don't want to do is develop a solution that cripples the process or worse, the business.

It's time to take back control of your business. My Lean Business Coach – Simply doing business

The nit picker

We've all seen them and worked with them, the nit-picker. The person who looks at something and finds fault in every way. Looking for quality is definitely not a bad thing; we all need to look at whatever it is we do and ensure the quality of work meets the expectations set and the customer requirements. What I'm talking about here is the person who ignores the value or the content and finds a fault with something most would regard as insignificant.

Let me give an example; when a report is written for a proposal (internal only) and you hand it in to a committee. They read through the report and provide feedback on the proposal and every point highlighted comes back with slight syntax adjustments, colour changes etc. Basically just presentation changes rather than content. Now this could mean that your content was spot on, and hopefully that is the case, however when this continues and the feedback is consistent in this regard you have to think they are skipping the content and looking primarily at the presentation.

So how do we respond to this? We are not doing ourselves or our business any favours by accepting and assuming the content is perfect, so I always have a conversation with the receiver to determine whether they are a nit-picker or not. With myself, if I am reviewing something I will provide a response that includes some mention of the content even if it is a positive review so that the creator knows that the content was considered and reviewed. Now, saying all of that we should endeavour to provide high quality work so that the receivers do not find anything to nit-pick and therefore will focus on the content.

Nit-picking isn't just a work thing either, take a look at how you respond to your family and friends. How many unnecessary arguments have you had in your life due to this? Hopefully none, but if you have, there is something you can do about it.

Less with more

Ok, so this week's post may seem a little counter intuitive to lean. How can your lean journey result in doing less with more? Surely that's a typo right? Isn't lean about doing more with less?

Wrong on all accounts. It is often said that lean is doing more with less, and while this can be an outcome it should never be your reason for starting your lean journey. Your reason for starting your lean journey should be around one of the following:

- Improve your customer experience, engagement and satisfaction
- Improve safety, morale and employee engagement
- Improve product quality, efficiency, productivity and profits

Those three cover just about every reason a business would want to start off on their lean journey and when effectively implemented all of the above can and should be achieved.

But what if when you start on your journey you have previously gone through a cost cutting restructure that so many businesses go through. It's possibly and even likely that after the cost cutting process the business was left with too few resources to efficiently provide the product or service to the customer. Lean shows us that there is an optimum resource level for every process and through the application of standardised work and kaizen we will define this optimum resource level. As regular readers will know, one of my pet frustrations is hearing people say "we've got to do more with less, let's go lean". That approach will often strangle a business into a slow (or fast) decline. With cost cutting comes a reduction in quality, safety, efficiency, productivity, customer satisfaction and profit!

It's because of all of this that I say when you start on your lean journey you have to trust where it takes you, don't go in with preconceived ideas of where it will take you. It may result in streamlined processes with fewer resources, but it may just as often result in streamlined processes with increased resources. And in the end, as long as the results are there and the business is strong and sustainable with happy, returning customers and safe, engaged employees what else matters?

Technology in your business

Technology, software solutions and applications are shouted about as the new dawn. While we are in the Information Age, we may often think we are in fact in the Technology Age as these systems keep popping up promising to revolutionise our businesses. While many of these systems can be of enormous benefit to a business and its people many (even the good ones) can strangle a business. And the system itself is very rarely to blame.

I have been asked on many occasions to be involved in or to conduct a post implementation review of new software systems, apps or technology as the business hasn't realised the expected benefits months and sometimes even years later. So why haven't the expectations been met? There is a very common thread in the answer to this question.

Often the first step businesses take when investigating a new system is contact a solution provider. This approach may be fine for a simple application that is used as a small part of an existing process; this may be used for documenting or capturing data. However when the software is more integrated as in the case of an Enterprise Resource Planning (ERP) Materials Resource Planning (MRP) Financial Accounting Package type of solution this approach is a big mistake. There are many other applications and software where this approach is not the right approach.

So how should a business go about this?

1) Well the very first step is to define the objective of the implementation. What problems is the business wanting to solve with the new technology. If there isn't a problem or constraint to be solved why are you going down this path?

2) The next step is to assign resources to the project. Yes that's right, this is a project. The project team should then develop a project plan.

3) The first real step is to determine the business needs. This is a detailed documentation of the requirements. The best way to achieve this is to map out the processes that the system will be capturing. A mistake many make is to buy a product in the hope that it will define the processes and controls for them. The business should already have defined processes prior to making a purchasing decision.

4) Make a list of prioritised requirements from step 3.

5) Go to market, see what options are out there to meet your requirements. This is where you will benefit from your earlier hard work.

6) Identify the most suitable option. Which solution has the closest match to your business requirements; this will include cost, ease of use, support as well as the requirements identified in step 3.

7) This is the biggest step; implementation. Take your time, don't rush it through. Resource the implementation effectively to ensure a good result.

Follow this up with a robust post implementation review.

Don't think that it's now over though, just about every system requires some sort of maintenance.

The value of the value stream map

Value Stream Mapping or VSM is a tool used in business improvement to help the business visualize its processes and waste and can be used as an alternative or to supplement Standardized Work. The VSM will achieve a couple of things:

1) Display the process logically from left to right

2) Identify and display the waste, incidental and value adding times of the processes

A VSM can be used to capture the entire business process or can be used to capture a specific part of the business and is normally used to capture the current state before improvements and the future state during the development of improvement plans.

The steps to creating a current state VSM are:

1) Determine the scope of the VSM

2) Observe and capture the times of the process elements. This can be done with a process study

3) Transfer the process onto the VSM sheet from left to right adding in inventory, transfer methods, inspection points etc.

4) Draw in the timeline under the process elements. Process operation times are recorded on the high points and waiting, transport are recorded on the low points

5) Display the total value add time as a percentage of the total lead time

There you have it, the Value Stream Map. Take a look at 7 Steps To A Lean Business for a more detailed instruction.

Communication

Communication, what does it mean? Is it different for every business?

Well, yes and no really. Communication in business is all about making sure everyone within your business knows and understands what they should and need to. There are a number of different reasons to communicate in a business, these include:

- Performance reporting of teams or individuals

- Company performance reporting

- Strategic communication

When designing your communication plan you need to determine:

- Who needs to be informed?

- What do they need to know?

- When do they need to know it?

- Importantly, why do they need to know it?

Within a business, different people will require different communication at different times; and this can be the same information. My approach has always been to tell my teams everything I can as soon as I can. Many managers only tell their teams what they want them to know; this is a very closed way of communicating and does not encourage clear two way communication and trust.

A simple method of developing the communications strategy is to develop a matrix with the top headings being:

- What

- When

- Why (what they will do with the information)

Down the left side, list all of the groups to receive the communication. Then fill in the corresponding information into the empty spaces to complete your plan.

When you get communication wrong, it often goes unnoticed until it's too late but when you get it right, it gets noticed at once!

What is in your control?

This is an interesting question, and you may be wondering why I am asking this question on a Lean Business blog. Whatever role we play in an organisation, all we can have an impact on directly are those things that we can control.

It is easy to become tied up and emotionally connected or bought into concerns that are outside of your control. This can be in your business, at work, not for profit or in your personal life.

Five reasons why you should only spend your resources on what you can control:

- You only have a limited amount of time, spend it wisely. Spending ones time is an interesting phrase; we often forget that time is the one resource we cannot make/find more of.

- You are taking the learning opportunity away from someone else. Who should be connecting with this issue? By taking over and investing your own resources on it you are taking away a learning opportunity from someone else.

- You end up owning the problem and the outcome. If you take over the issue, not only does the problem become yours to fix, but the outcome whether good or bad becomes your to own also.

- What are the opportunity costs? What else should you be working on that you do have control over and what are the costs (whether financial or other)?

- What else in your life does it affect? Further to the above, what other parts of your life are being impacted? Are the costs of working on something you cannot control too great?

What does all of this have to do with lean business? The purpose of lean is to ensure every part of the organisation is working at its peak efficiency. If we are not working on what we have control over we and the greater organisation are not working efficiently.

The epiphany

The aha moment, when the light bulb goes on. We've all had them, or have we? I was listening to someone recently commenting on when they had their aha moment and realised as they were talking that this person had never actually had one. They thought they had, but hadn't and it got me thinking.

If you've never had an epiphany, you won't know that you haven't had one. Regardless of what the epiphany is about, when you have one you will know. You'll be like a kid in a candy shop, uncontrollable delight, dancing in the street.

I've had two epiphany moments in my life, one when I truly understood my calling and the other when I understood lean and how it could improve the businesses I worked for and with. Just about every day since my lean aha moment I have been applying the tools and philosophies whether at work, at home or in leisure. It's become what I do and a little of

When I see people who say they have had the aha moment with lean and they don't practice it, I know they haven't really had the epiphany. They need more time or more help to really "see" otherwise why wouldn't they practice it every day? It sounds like a religion rather than a business philosophy but that's how infectious lean is when it is really understood.

So look at the people you are working with, how many of them had really had the aha moment? What can you do to help them "see"?

Collaboration

Is collaboration an important behaviour to have in business? I believe collaboration is an underestimated must have for successful businesses and project implementation. What does collaboration mean? Dictionary.com defines collaboration as 'the act of working with another or others on a joint project'.

Collaboration is the very reason we employ staff and teams within any business; if all of the work could be achieved by a single operator there would be no need for staff right? But collaboration takes having staff to another level as it multiplies the value when working well.

What do I mean by multiplying the value? If you have a single person working on a project you have value x 1

If you add two more people to the team and they are working independently you have value x 3. So the value received from the team is simply the number in the team x 1; this is not good value for your investment and does not give great results. You want great results don't you?

When you have a team working collaboratively the equation looks more similar to this: value = team(n) squared. So in the example of a team of three, value =3x3.

Now this is not a guaranteed outcome, however, when you have a well balanced and collaborative team working on a focused result this is not only achievable but likely. So, just how do you create this team?

- Employ the right people
    - Look for teamwork and attitude over technical aptitude
- Clearly define the project goals
    - The clearer these are the better the outcomes will be
- Provide focus
    - FOCUS stands for – Follow One Course Until Success
- Don't spread them too thin
    - Let them get on with bringing you success

Your one thing

I am currently reading a book written by Gary Keller and Jay Papasan titled "The One Thing" and it has me thinking not only about my One Thing that I should be focusing on but the very fact that I often think about far too many things, too often.

I've been doing some reflection and realize that I am far more effective and achieve more when I am not multi-tasking and can focus on one or very few tasks at a time. I find I do need some level of disruption to perform at my best, so I often do try and do too many things at once.

The secret, at least for me, is to do one thing at a time. However, by having a controlled number of things going on and switching between them regularly to allow the subconscious mind to be active in the background and create the solutions. But this is what works best for me.

The secret for you may be the same, but it's likely to be different. The secret for you is to find out what works best for you and this can only be achieved through trial and error and reflection. Just like the PDCA (Plan, Do, Check, Act) cycle used for your business processes, you can use the same process to understand your optimum working method and cycle.

With this knowledge, here's what I have done to keep myself on track and support my optimum style.

- I have shortened my To Do list
    - I now only have 5 things on my list. I tried 1 but just could cope with the singular focus
- I keep these 5 things in my visible view during my working time
    - This helps keep me focused on the 5 and keeps other things from breaking into my field
- I assess it regularly
    - If something needs to be added, something else needs to come off

Give it a go, if I can do it, anyone can.

Lean success

What does success in your lean journey look like? That's a great question and an easy one to answer. Many people would say things like:

- Sustained 5S
- Kanban systems in place
- Standardized work being followed
- Built in quality and poka yoke

This is all true but does NOT mean you have a successful lean business I'm afraid. These are all just tools that can be used to help your business succeed and are a part of the 'Lean Toolkit'.

Success in a lean business looks just like success in every business. You do not successfully implement lean or "do 5S" or any of the other lean tools. Lean is a journey that is never ending. If your business is achieving its business goals, with satisfied customers and staff, then you are successful; simple. If you have all of the tools in use but are still not achieving your business goals, then you are not as successful; and there are limitless levels of both success and failure in business.

So what makes it a success? Lean should not be an add-on toolkit, your lean business systems should be embedded into your management system and your culture (also known as "the way we do things around here"). This will only happen by strong leadership and aligned goals and objectives with supportive KPI's.

Only when it is truly embedded can you say your lean journey is being successful, as for your business, are you successful?

The three pillars of business success

What are the three necessary philosophies for a business to achieve total success? If these three philosophies are believed and lived, any business can be successful. The only prerequisite is that the business must have a product or service that is in demand and must have a customer base or share of a market.

Philosophy Number 1 - Respect, believe in and support your people.

There are couple of major aspects of this philosophy.
- First and foremost, you have to provide a safe workplace for your people. This includes physical, mental and emotional safety.
- Ensure availability of resources to do the tasks. This includes plant, tooling and people.
- Provide a fair and equitable management culture. Hold everyone equally accountable and don't overuse the stars in your teams.

Philosophy Number 2 - Be in touch with your customers and give them what they want.

- At the end of the day, if you don't have customers you simply don't have a business (you have a hobby). Ask your customers what they want; this must be sincere. If you ask and don't follow through you will be caught out!

- Don't fall into the trap of over-promises. This is an easy trap to get caught in when you are trying to please. No-one wins from over-promising.
- Know when to say no. Sometimes it just isn't worth doing and there is nothing wrong knowing when it's the right time to say "thanks, but no thanks".

Philosophy Number 3 – Have a focus on quality. Do things right the first time.

There are three good reasons why doing it right first time is the best way of doing business.

- Your customers do not want to pay for rework or have to return faulty products due to poor processes.
- Your employees don't want to waste their time doing things twice. Believe it or not, your employees come to work to do the right thing, it's up to you to set the example and create robust repeatable processes.
- Your bank balance. It costs money to do things twice, or three times. Every time rework is performed in your business it is impacting your profit.

How well do you measure up against the three things?

Productivity or efficiency?

Lately, I have been hearing a lot about productivity and efficiency and need to clarify a couple of things. "We're working on improving our efficiency" is a common statement from a lot of businesses and business leaders. Improving efficiency is an effective way of removing the waste from your processes and potentially increasing your margins; if you aren't being productive though, does it really make much difference?

Productivity in its simplest form is just a measure of time allocated to actual work. So out of an 8 hour day, if you are working for 6 hours you are productive 75% of the time. You may have 2 hours for meetings, breaks or other non-productive activities. To improve profit margin, you make those 6 hours more productive by being more efficient; well that's how we're taught it works, right? Not quite right!

So what is efficiency? You are efficient when you have removed waste from your activity and are spending as much time on the productive activity you are working on.

The problem with the above scenario is you can work on making yourself and your business more efficient at doing the wrong things. There is no mention of value or the customer!

We have to change the way we look at productivity; it isn't merely doing work, it is adding value for the customer. When we look at productivity as an activity that adds value to whatever it is the customer is getting out of the transaction, we have a good base to start from. When we have our teams working on the right things as much as possible (high productivity) we can work on increasing the efficiency and begin removing waste the processes.

What is inside the word productivity? Productive. Are you and your teams productive?

Two out of three

Good, Fast, Cheap; in project management training I was taught you can only ever expect two out of three of these. You can do good and fast, but it won't be cheap. You can do good and cheap, but it won't be fast; and you can do fast and cheap, but it won't be good. At the time, I took a little convincing (mostly because I like a challenge) but in the end I subscribed to this 'fact'.

But what about in business generally? Can a customer expect a good product, fast and cheap? Should a business try and achieve all three? Or is it a recipe for disaster? I've put up a couple of variations of the below pic on my twitter feed over the last couple of months and it's created a bit of debate so I thought I'd discuss the concept further in a blog.

Now, all three of the aspects are subjective so will probably mean something different to different people, depending on a number of factors. But I still believe achieving all three is not sustainable. As a customer I often take this into account when making my buying decisions. As a businessman I take this into account at every stage in the business planning and value delivery process.

Let's look at why this is truth exists. Take any product or service and break down the process of creating value, whatever line of business you are in. To create value costs money; let's look at a simple cookie company process.

To make cookies you have to purchase raw material such as flour, eggs, milk solids, water, sugar, salt etc. Then you need labour and other resources such as power and gas and manufacturing equipment. This all costs money; and the better quality the raw materials and greater skilled and number of staff the higher the cost.

So already, to make better quality cookies you need better quality raw materials which will likely result in the product not being cheap. If you want to produce them fast, you need good quality, well trained employees and good quality ovens and equipment; once again this will add cost and result in your product being 'not cheap'.

If you want cheap cookies, you will use lower quality raw materials and / or lower paid employees and equipment. Resulting in either low quality product or slow delivery.

Good, Fast, Cheap. Choose which 2 you want to delivery, because you can't deliver all three!

Perfectionism or procrastination?

Is your perfectionism holding you back, or are you simply a procrastinator? Procrastination has been around for a long, long time. As humans, we have the ability to think and consider the future. This is obviously a great strength of our species, but for some it can lead to procrastination. So what is the difference between these two?

Perfectionism, according to dictionary.com u: a personal standard, attitude or philosophy that demands perfection and rejects anything less. An Americanism from 1830-1840 with no known lineage.

Procrastination, according to dictionary.com means: to put off to delay, especially something requiring immediate attention. First used in English in the 1540's from Middle French, the term is derived from Latin *'procratinationem'* of unknown origin.

Looking at the two meanings, it is not hard to see why many people have 'converted' from being a procrastinator to a perfectionist; but I think most 'perfectionists' are in fact procrastinators in disguise! Holding out on the release of a product, project, process or anything because you want to make sure it's perfect before releasing is not perfectionism, it's procrastination and it is holding back you and your business. Follow the PDCA cycle and test (do) early to give feedback (check). This will speed up the development process. The main reason people procrastinate is a lack of confidence; if you measure your value by how good your first iteration is you're missing the whole point. Measure the value of your product by the last iteration, not the first.

As Reid Hoffman, the founder of Linkedin is quoted "If you are not embarrassed by the first version of your product, you've launched too late". Obviously this must be followed up with fast response and iterations to feedback.

So what are you? A perfectionist or a procrastinator?

It's the results that matter

I read quite a few blogs and forums, a number of which are on business and the many streams of business improvement. The number one thing that makes me turn away from a site is the arguing and bickering over which stream is the better and the put downs by some, of another person's deviation from the "pure" process.

For the first point, as a proponent and student of TPS, a Six Sigma Master Black Belt and a 20 year veteran of Quality Systems I think I am in a good position have an opinion on the matter. Most of the people who do argue probably will not like my opinion though as I don't believe any of the business improvement streams are better than any others. It really depends on a couple of factors:

- Firstly, it really depends on the situation and the problem at hand as to which can provide the best solution
- Secondly, it depends on the culture of the business as each of the different streams work best with certain management types and business structures
- And lastly, it depends greatly on the experience and training of the lead practitioner and their team

Now for the second point; to achieve the best results from your business improvement activities you have to know a couple of things:

1) You need a defined problem
2) You need to understand your business improvement process

If you really understand your business improvement processes you will know that all of the tools in any of the streams are really guides. The very people who designed them and used them during their development, designed them to be flexible to suit the situation and circumstances of their use. The core structure of the process is defined, but the finer points should be moulded to suit the problem, the people and the environment. Those who get the best results across different businesses always do this. It's what I call "real word learning".

Those that insist on arguing are forgetting something; what really matters surely must be the results achieved! If we put the purity of the process over the results achieved we are missing the whole point of improvement – to achieve our goals!

Supplier relationships

What type of relationship do you have with your suppliers? Is it a simple buyer and seller relationship with transactions made with anonymity over the phone or internet? Or do you enjoy a partnership with your suppliers?

Over my time in business I have been a supplier, customer and 3rd party and have dealt with people of all types. When working as a supplier to the automotive industry, I enjoyed the partnership of working with the likes of Toyota, the highly monitored relationship of supplying to Ford and the big stick approach of Holden (GM).

By shopping around for the best price you can save yourself some good coin in the short term, but you can never be too sure of the level of service or quality you are going to get in return. The cheaper price in the short term can and often does end up costing you more.

Most of the benefits of a partner relationship with your suppliers are soft; however the medium to long term benefits can definitely save you money, time and maybe most importantly, reputation. Without a good reputation your business will struggle to grow or even survive and the role your suppliers play in developing and maintaining your reputation should not be underestimated.

Other benefits of a true partnership with your suppliers:

- Reliable supply
    - Without reliable supply you cannot be efficient as you will be forced to change your plan due to shortages
- Consistent quality
    - This has a couple of benefits. Firstly, similar to above, with poor quality comes poor efficiency.
    - Secondly, your after-sales costs will increase due to poor reliability.
- On call – you cannot put a price to having a supplier that will go above and beyond when you need it most. When you have an urgent requirement and you have a supplier you can trust and who feels a part of your business, they will come to the rescue!

As well as all of this, you may just have a friendship too. And friendships in business are just too rare.

Are you a hider or a seeker?

This is not the childhood game of hide and seek we're talking about here, this is business. In business there are three types of people;

- Those that hide from problems, not wanting to know what is really going on in the business. These are the hiders of your business.
- Those that seek out problems and challenge the status quo.
  - You guessed it, these are the seekers.
- And those who don't care either way and just go with the flow. These are the dead fish – from the old unclaimed quote "only dead fish go with the flow".

Which is best for your business? And which are you?

As a business improvement specialist, the first thing I do when I walk into the business is see who is who. For the journey to be successful you can have a mixture of all three types, and you often do. What is critical though, is where in the business they sit.

In leadership roles, it is absolutely critical you have seekers for your business improvement journey to be successful. Now I'm not saying a business full of hiders will fail, some will not and some will, there are many factors. But if you are serious about starting on and finishing a business improvement journey, you'll need seekers in the key leadership roles.

From a business improvement point of view, of the three types, the hider is the worst. The hider does not want to know what is really happening and often hide behind talking about opportunities and positive speak in the face of big challenges. They won't necessarily not want to fix things, they often just don't know how big the issues are and are often shocked when the entire problem is laid out in front of them with facts.

The dead fish actually isn't too bad as they just don't know any better and can often quite easily be turned into seekers when their eyes are opened to the opportunities before them. If they aren't turned into seekers and remain as dead fish, they will usually go with wherever the flow takes them; if this is on an improvement journey then all the better.

So ask yourself two questions; which type are you? And; which type are your leaders?

Meetings; destructive or constructive

Last week I attended a conference in Melbourne; being a manufacturing efficiency conference the talk was mostly about improving productivity and efficiency in a manufacturing environment. Something I am very passionate about.

One of the things that really stuck in my mind was the amount of talk about meetings and importantly, their impact on productivity. One of the speakers called meetings "the ultimate productivity killer!" Now I don't know if I agree 100%, but I do know too many businesses spend too much time in meetings. True to the lean way, I decided to go through the 5 why's to find out what the causes of all of these meetings are.

Assessing the many businesses I have been involved with shows a couple of consistencies.

Some businesses use meetings in a positive, constructive manner by holding meetings primarily for the purpose of information dissemination or communication of important information. This can be done before a decision, to "sell" an idea to superiors, to gain the support of peers or to simply gather other opinions of an idea or concept. They also hold meetings after a decision to share the decision and the outcomes to those impacted, or to share knowledge through the business. These businesses tend to hold fewer meetings for shorter periods to assist with the communication.

Other businesses, may do some of the above, but also use meetings to actually make decisions. Some people actually use meetings in an effort to get others to make their decisions for them. Let me be clear, major or minor decisions should not be made in meetings. What you will get is group think, so while you may be trying to have a majority decision, you are unlikely to get this result.

You can tell what type of business you are in just by observing any meeting. In a business using meetings effectively, people will bring results of investigations, knowledge and answers to the meetings. In businesses using meetings ineffectively, people will bring questions and not much more to the meetings. The worst type of meetings are those where the topics are discussed by a large group; the discussion should have already happened, and the decision tabled. That's it, simple! Meetings are not for long discussions, if you need more people involved, hold a workshop with only those required.

Businesses spend way too much time in meetings; after conducting the 5 whys, I have concluded a big part of the problem is people's inability to make a decision. They want others to assist or even make the decision for them. It may be better than procrastination, but it's still a massive inefficiency in business. Which type of business is yours?

A great place to work!

Yesterday I read the list of "Best Places To Work in Australia" from the BRW list and it got me thinking; what makes a great place to work?

Is it money? There have been countless studies over the years to debunk this myth. Sure, money is important and we all like to be remunerated appropriately, however the fact is that most businesses that pay more to pick up the superstars have a higher than average staff turnover. This doesn't mean you can pay less though; remuneration is a factor, albeit a smaller one.

What about working hours? Another myth, working less hours does not lead to happier employees. Conversely, working more hours does not necessarily lead to unhappy employees. It's all about what they do in the time your staff are there and how flexible the working arrangements are. Most employees don't mind working late to get through any urgent and critical work, but do mind having to work to a time when all of their work is done. It should be a two way street.

How about the perks? This is an interesting topic; perks can come in many different guises. From extra holidays, to dinners with family, the list is endless. Perks are a good way to reward and recognise your employees. Make sure they are personal though; giving everyone a fuel voucher doesn't really tick this box. Giving a perk that impacts the family of your employees also makes a huge difference; remember, when your employee's do that little bit extra for you and your business, they are doing less with their family. So show you really appreciate it and reward the whole family where you can!

Culture. This is the winner; what makes an organisation a great place to work is the culture! Reading through the list from BRW, culture was the clear winner. It wasn't solely about the money, or the hours, or the perks; it was about the culture.

What makes a good culture? Good cultures don't just happen; they are created, nurtured and are always growing. The single biggest factor in creating a good culture is **honestly** respecting and valuing your team. People work it out very quickly if you're not sincere; you can't fake this. There are many examples of ways to do this from table tennis tables in the lunch room, to paid holidays and everything in between; but the absolute key is for your team to know you sincerely care about them and their families.

The place of realism in problem solving

In my profession I believe it is always best to know the reality of a situation. This means asking about, talking about and bringing up problems and issues. This is often seen as negativity, but I actually see it as reality and as a follow on from my recent blog *Are You A Hider or a Seeker* I'll expand on this a little here.

The following is a simple 5 step problem solving process I use everywhere I go. It works and is trusted.

Step 1)

    Define the problem

Step 2)

    Provide evidence of the problem. This includes current state and historical data analysis

Step 3)

    Root cause analysis of the problem

Step 4)

    Develop corrective actions

Step 5)

    Test and validate. Return to earlier steps if necessary.

A simple process, but a process that only works when the problem is defined. This brings us back to where we started; to improve, we must acknowledge and understand our problems otherwise we will not be in a position to fix them. Don't find problems where they don't exist, but do not hide away and ignore them. They will not go away, they will eventually cause some harm somewhere in the system.

So how do you find the problems? Genchi Genbutsu, go and see; speak to those doing the tasks and ask questions to find out what causes them issues. Simple, but it doesn't happen by itself!

The comfort zone

There is an old poem called *My Comfort Zone*; the author is unknown unfortunately, but it is a great piece of work that I often go back to whenever I need a reminder. I try and push myself outside my comfort zone regularly, but from time to time, I find myself falling back into old habits and staying put right in my own comfort zone.

I used to have a comfort zone where I knew I wouldn't fail.
The same four walls and busywork were really more like jail.
I longed so much to do the things I'd never done before,
But stayed inside my comfort zone and paced the same old floor.
I said it didn't matter that I wasn't doing much.
I said I didn't care for things like commission checks and such.
I claimed to be so busy with the things inside the zone,
But deep inside I longed for something special of my own.
I couldn't let my life go by just watching others win.
I held my breath; I stepped outside and let the change begin.
I took a step and with new strength I'd never felt before,
I kissed my comfort zone goodbye and closed and locked the door.
If you're in a comfort zone, afraid to venture out,
Remember that all winners were at one time filled with doubt.
A step or two and words of praise can make your dreams come true.
Reach for your future with a smile; success is there for you!

The comfort zone is two things; it's is a safe house for those too frightened to step outside. It gives them a sense of security, of knowing what may lie ahead without fear of the unknown. Secondly, the comfort zone is a challenge to be taken up by those who are up to it. Stepping over that comfort zone line can be both an anxious and exhilarating moment; one that can literally change your life.

There are comfort zones in every aspect of one's life; in business, in personal life with relationships and individual aspects. What is important is that you don't take the challenge for the wrong reasons; remember, this is **your** comfort zone – step out of it for **your** reasons, to challenge and improve **your** life, not someone else's.

So go for it, take that first step outside your comfort zone and do it with gusto!

One out all out

This week's blog is a little different; it's not about lean, but rather about a trend I am seeing more and more of that is hurting our economies.

Last week I was chatting to a builder who is doing some renovations in my home. Chatting about this and that and we got onto a story of his from his days working on high rises in the city. Here is a short replication of the story:

"We were working on a massive high rise in Melbourne and I was on the office fit-out side of the project. The building was at lock-up stage so all of the glass was in and the air conditioning was working. It was during summer (for those not familiar Melbourne summers, it will often reach 40°C during the summer months) and the forecast for the day was a pretty warm one. We were working away inside the building, so we had the air-conditioning set at a nice 22°C and we were getting through our work. As the temperature raised and approached 35° we were informed we would be "downing tools" once it reached 35° as per the working agreement. As we knew it would, just after lunch, the temperature was reached and we all went home with full pay. This went on for the next week or so."

This occurs every year in this state and right across Australia and the world. Now don't misunderstand, I am all for, and often the first person to stand up for safe working conditions for all workers; however to send home hundreds of workers who are working in 22°air-conditioned comfort because the outside temperature is too high is absolutely ridiculous! This one out, all out policy needs to change for businesses to remain viable otherwise jobs will be lost in the long term.

I make no effort to hide the fact that I don't understand the role of Unions in today's world (at least in the developed world); but this goes beyond not understanding and takes it to another level. To send home workers who want to work goes against good business and borders on industrial sabotage. The Unions have to become more commercially minded to remain relevant in a highly competitive global economy.

Sometimes you just don't win

What a big weekend of football grand finals; Saturday, a big win by the mighty Hawthorn Hawks in Melbourne in the AFL and Sunday, a come from behind overtime win by North Qld in the NRL. Two big games to great wins achieved in two entirely different ways. What does this have to do with business? Well I didn't speak of the two losers did I? So were the two winners the best teams? Results would suggest yes; but not necessarily. Yes, they scored the most points to win the match but there are many elements that must come together to win.

Just like sport, there are winners and losers in most transactions. Rarely is a business the only one offering a proposal. So what makes the difference between the winners and the losers? And what should you do if you are a recent loser?

Firstly, what is the difference? Well, both of these teams were hungrier for the win than their opponents. In the close NRL game, the losing side was leading for most of the match; in fact it wasn't until the last second of the match North Qld tied the match after trailing for much of the game.

Just like sport, in business it isn't always the best that wins. I'm sure you've seen those who you are better than, smarter than, more experienced than, yet they seem to win? Why is that? Do they give up or do they persevere until the final whistle blows? What about you? Do you keep pushing until the very end or are you easily distracted, put off by a small issue? To win, you must play and play til the very end.

How do you come back from a loss? The first thing is to analyse and understand why you lost. You should not change anything without evidence to show why you lost. Whether it is in sport, in business or any other part of your life you need to know why you lost before you can change the process.

Once you understand why you lost you can then go about modifying what you do (the process) to effect the outcome. This is the Plan, Do, Check, Act cycle and is applicable to any and every process.

It's also a good idea to understand why you win, so you can build in repeatability.

So, to be a winner you have to be hungry, go after the win and analyse the results from your processes.

Clear strategy

I recently spent a day working on a strategic plan with a local NFP community organisation. It was a good day with all of the Directors present working through the strategic plan; breaking it down into actions and assigning responsibilities as you would normally do. It was a fairly unstructured approach, however we did achieve quite a lot.

The achievement was possible only because we knew what the vision was. The strategic plan was clear and everyone participating understood what the vision looked like, for the most part; importantly, when some clarity was required, the answer could be easily communicated.

I was involved with another group recently of a similar organisation type. This group had a strategic plan that wasn't quite as well structured or understood. The difference between the two sessions was massive; yet the planned outcome was the same. This group spent most of the session understanding and agreeing on what the strategic plan actually looked like. In reality, this group was trying to break down the plan before it was ready. Seeing this first hand, I thought I would provide a quick guide on how to develop and process your strategic plan.

1) Develop the plan
    a) This is done with many inputs and should never be solely a top down approach. The leader needs

to share their vision and work with the group to develop that vision into a plan.

      b) My approach is to use brainstorming, multi voting or other tools to develop the plan

2) Gain consensus

      a) If you haven't got consensus from the team owning the plan it will never work

      b) Encourage the team to challenge or ask for clarity for any points they don't agree with or understand

3) Take a break a let everyone get clear

      a) You cannot go straight from making the plan into the next steps; take a break to give everyone time to get clear on what the plan means

4) Break the plan down into actionable items

5) Assign responsibilities and timeframes

6) Review regularly

It's pretty simple to develop, rollout and work through a strategic plan. Where most businesses go wrong is they aren't clear enough in the plan itself and leave far too much open to interpretation. Now, if you're too specific you will stifle creativity but not specific enough means too much indecision; you need to balance this with the capabilities and personalities of the team. One size does not fit all!

Tenacity

"The quality or fact of being very determined; determination" Dictionary.com

Are you tenacious? Or does a lack of persistence cost you success?

I watched a movie on a recent flight interstate; there was not much worth watching on the inflight system so I chose a movie that was short so I could have a sleep before landing. I chose *Unfinished Business*; a comedy with a very poor review rating. I often find myself enjoying movies that rate poorly with others so am not put off by bad reviews.

Well, the movie was funny in places; however the sub story in the background was what I found most enjoyable and actually inspiring. It came as quite a surprise to find myself being inspired by a poorly rating comedy flick but I guess inspiration can come from many different places.

What was inspiring about the story was the tenacity the main character and his small team showed to succeed, pushing through every barrier put up in front of them. Now, I know this is just a movie; and some of the barriers were pretty unrealistic, but I can only assume the many poor reviews came from viewers who did not grasp the sub story.

We are all faced with the decision to stop or keep pressing ahead in all parts of our lives; this is our own test of tenacity and is a test we should take seriously. Being persistent is a trait found in many of the world's most successful people regardless of their endeavour. You never pick up a biography of a successful person and read "it was really easy to get here; I just woke up one day and found success?" No, what you will find is a long and arduous road to success; often with many mountains to climb and ravines to clamber out of.

Take a look at your own journey, how many times have you persevered through the difficult challenges to find success at the end? How many times have you given up too early and held regrets?

There must come a time though when you have to say "enough is enough". To persevere when the likelihood of succeeding is just as painful a lesson as to give up too soon and no-one can tell when or where this tipping point is.

Customer issues

How does your business deal with its customer issues? Every business has them at some point in time; no business is absolutely free from complaints.

The manner in which you manage your customer complaints really can make or break your business. A positive outcome and stronger relationship with a customer can be the end result when a customer complaint is handled effectively.

Conversely, a strained relationship can result if the situation is handled poorly. Let me give you an example. I recently had to call my energy company to make a complaint about a certain part of the service. We all know how frustrating it can be waiting and talking to a telco or energy provider. I was on hold waiting and becoming a little more frustrated as the time went on. I was calling as I hadn't had a bill for a number of months and was now facing a significant bill to catch up. It was at my request they billed me otherwise I would have had to wait longer and had an even higher bill!

By the time I was hanging up the call, I was happy to the point of wanting to recommend others to use this company. How did the operator turn a frustrated, agitated customer into a happy, satisfied customer? The first thing was sincerity; the operator seemed sincere and showed empathy when discussing the issue. The next thing was they did what they promised; there is nothing worse as a customer to come to an agreement on a way forward only to have the supplier/provider renege. Lastly, they sincerely thanked me for my contact, apologised and provided me some level of confidence the issue would be resolved.

Some businesses I have worked with and have been a customer of see a customer complaint differently and will do everything possible to either not answer or not help the customer. This will only ever result in a customer base that will leave as soon as a better (or even just different) option becomes available in the market.

It is important to see the complaint as an opportunity to provide a better experience for the customer; not all customers complain, many just don't come back. Those that do complain care enough to do so; so don't waste the opportunity.

Where do I start?

Should I start with 5S, Standardised Work or Kaizen? I get this question quite a lot from business owners and managers alike. Well, the correct answer is supposed to be to start with 5S; this is the way Toyota do things; and I can't say I've ever really gone wrong by following their way.

The reason why they start with 5S is because it teaches you and readies you for all that will follow in Standardised Work, Kaizen, Jidoka etc. It also brings a level of control and discipline to the process. What they don't say is implement a 5S system across the entire business or value stream before doing anything else; and this is where many people have got their meaning wrong.

That's why I like to start off with a value stream map first to understand and define the current state process. This also helps identify where the current bottlenecks are and areas needing the most urgent improvement. Here is the process I follow with every business that is successful in its lean journey.

1) Construct current state value stream map
    Capture the data using timing studies, combination charts, process study or other methods
2) Analyse current state and conduct gap analysis
    Compare current state to your specific goals to identify gaps and opportunities

3) Identify areas for opportunity

This is where the lean / TPS tools come into play. In the areas you have identified get started with 5S to bring some discipline and standardisation to the work space. This is followed by kaizen and standardised work to bring tangible improvements to the process. When accompanied by Jidoka and JIT systems you will have a world class process when complete.

Moving onto the next process can and should be started when still working on the previous process; this will make the journey faster and will create synergy between processes.

I like to start working at the end process and work backwards through the value stream rather than start with bottlenecks. This is a little slower to bring big benefits, however does provide better benefits in the long term.

For more info visit us at www.mlbc.com.au and see our free video tutorials.

Why, why, why

We've all heard of the 5 Why's and most of us use it as a tool in our workplaces to assist with identifying root causes. But are we using it correctly and really getting down to the root cause? Or are we stopping the questioning too early or too late?

For those that aren't aware, here is a quick introduction to the 5 Whys process.

When identifying why something has occurred, we call this root cause analysis. One of the favourite tools is the 5 Why's and comes from Toyota. It is a process of asking the question "why" until the real reason for the failure or the "root cause" is understood. AN example is below:

Problem: Fuse blown on wet saw.

Why? Pump overloaded.

Why? Lack of lubrication

Why? Pump pressure too low.

Why? Pump shaft is worn.

Why? Metal shavings are sucked up into pump.

Why? No filter on pump.

Without applying the 5 Why's the fuse would have been replaced over and over before it was realized that the lubrication was poor. This may have led to overfilling the lubrication reservoir or replacing the pump. When in fact the root cause was a lack of filter on the pump intake which could be a design defect, failure or maintenance issue.

If you stop short of identifying the root cause you will never fix the actual problem and will continue to spend time and money (waste) on fixing the symptoms. If you continue asking the question past the root cause that is controllable you will never really fix the issue as the mountain will be too great to climb. In the above example we could have continued and asked why there was no filter on the pump which would lead us to the machine manufacturer who would need to involve the pump manufacturer to redesign to include a pump (after much testing to prove a filter isn't needed). In reality a pump was fitted and the problem is solved; we could go to the machine manufacturer and share our learnings so they can make ongoing improvements to their machine of course!

So there you have it, the 5 Why's. How well do you use it?

KPI's that matter

How do you make sure the KPI's in your business really make a difference?

What is the purpose of a KPI? A key performance indicator as the name suggests is used to measure an important process or result within a business. A business or business unit may have many metrics that are used to ensure the day to day operations are functioning correctly, but most of these are not Key Performance Indicators; they are simply measures or quite often they are lead indicators.

A KPI should be linked to the bigger picture, or the strategic plan and needs to either answer a question or help with decision making. If it does neither of these two things then think about culling it.

I like to follow the SQDCM format for reporting my KPI's; it keeps the intention of the indicator clear and allows for easy communication and reporting.

Safety

Quality

Delivery

Cost

Morale

Believe it or not, every part of the business can measure what they do and their outputs against these headings; even support services such as IT, Human Resources and Finance.

Hoshin Kanri is a Japanese Term that is popular at the moment; similar to cascading down of the strategic plan and cascading up of the KPI's and other metrics. This allows every employee to understand how their work helps the business achieve its strategic objectives. Cascading objectives and KPI's can be a challenge to set up, however when used effectively can be a great benefit.

One last piece of advice, don't have too many KPI's. Too often I see businesses talk up their KPI, Planning and Reporting system only to see they have far too many metrics to manage and really analyse. Too many metrics leads to nothing being done with the data. If you aren't using it, cull it – this doesn't mean stop the data collection (unless it takes effort to collect) but it does mean stop the reporting and analysis.

What is your value stream?

As a carry-over from last week's blog; one of the comments I received back prompted me to discuss the value stream to clarify and make it simple for you all to define your own value streams. So firstly, what is a value stream?

Every business must create value in some way or another, it isn't always a product and these days it doesn't even really need to be a service as one would historically think of one. The only reality is, whatever your business does, it must create value of some sort for someone; otherwise you wouldn't be in business, or you must be running a business as a cover for illegal activities :)

Let's look at some business models and look at what value they provide.

Sandwich Shop:

The sandwich shop provides its customers with a convenient method of preparing a meal. It would be more cost effective for the customer to purchase bread, butter and fillings from the supermarket and make their own lunch at home; but customers of sandwich shops value their time and rather the convenience of not having to make it themselves and not having to shop for fresh bread and fillings.

Bakery:

In the past, every household would bake their own bread; now as you can see from the above example, many households don't even make their own sandwiches anymore. So the bakery (one of the world's oldest value streams) buys the ingredients and invests the capital and time to make bread for a community. This allows the community to free up their time and resources to bring value to the community in other ways.

Farmer:

The farmer (which is probably the oldest value stream; if you don't include the hunter gatherer era) grows wheat in enormous volumes to provide raw materials for the bakeries.

You could argue that from the farmer to the customer eating a sandwich is one value stream, however we break it into pieces for a couple of reasons:

> 1) To make mapping and reviewing more simple and manageable
> 2) To match the value stream with individual businesses or business units. If you did manage the entire value stream in a single business you would still break it down as it is highly likely each section would be a separate business unit with separate budgets etc.

Each value stream starts and stops at the points where each business starts and stops their involvement in the process. For instance, in the case of the farmer, they purchase seed, fertilizer and other consumables/inputs; the process of ordering, receiving, storing and planting are part of the value stream. Preparing the field for planting, along with growing, harvesting, storage, packaging and distribution (if they don't use a 3rd party) are all part of the value stream.

Take a look at your business and determine where your value stream starts and finishes. There are likely to be a number of branches; both inputs and outputs. It's important to map your value stream at different levels; both a macro and micro level to get the best results.

When to say 'enough is enough"

Persistence and tenacity are values observed in the world's most successful people; no matter how you manage success and no matter what vocation. These are two of the most important keys to success for you; however it is often forgotten or not mentioned that these same successful people say "no" and change direction so are not tenacious to the point of failing.

So how do you know it is time to say "enough is enough"? Well just like so many other things in life and business, it starts with how well you plan. Yes, that word again; you may get the impression that I am a fan of good planning if you're a regular reader.

A good business plan or project plan (I'll just call these all plans from now on) includes something called contingencies. All plans are developed with the best outcomes in mind, no one wants to fail, so our plans are focussed on succeeding; but from time to time, no matter how lucky we are or how hard we work, there are times when not everything will go to plan. This is when we need to have Plan B.

Plan B is what we do when things don't quite work out; a contingency plan. A good plan looks at what can feasibly go wrong at each step of the project, the risk is assessed and contingency plans developed for any high impact or high probability risks. You don't need to have a plan for every risk.

The greatest risk, is the risk of failure. You should include in your plan the point of no return, this is the point when you get the chance to continue or to exclaim "enough is enough" and stop the project. Far too many projects are dragged to completion that really should have been stopped at this point; often the team knows it, the project manager knows it, but no one says it.

Take a look back at some of your most recent projects, are there any you should have stopped in hindsight? Think about when you had the knowledge, or even the gut feeling that the outcome wasn't going to be there? Take this knowledge into your next project.

Process management

How often do you find processes get shortcut? This happens in many businesses and usually when the business gets busier or is in a hectic state. This is also when the business can least afford a shortcut to its processes as it often results in poor quality, late delivery and higher failure rates; which all results in unhappy customers.

So why does this happen? There are two reasons why a process will get shortcut:

1) The process doesn't work

When this occurs, you will find the process consistently being not followed because by following the process you will not achieve the desired outcome. This often occurs in mature, larger businesses where the work practice has outgrown the written process over time and the written process has not been updated. This also occurs when the process is documented by the wrong person; by this I mean a "desk top expert". When documenting a process you need to go to the Gemba.

If what is happening in reality works, is followed consistently and provides consistent good outcomes, you simply need to update your documentation to reflect the reality and you're done.

If what is happening still isn't right, then a review needs to take place with the agreed resulting process documented.

2) The process works but is cumbersome

In other words, it's easier, quicker and therefore accepted (when busy) to not follow the process than it is to follow the process. You'll find with this type of issue, when the business is not busy and has time to do the right thing, it generally will. But as soon as it gets hectic this is a process that will be shortcut.

So how do you stop this happening?

When developing or reworking a process I like to put it through a test and this is where I also like to follow the KISS principle. Keep It Super Simple!

A process should not be a burden to follow; make it as easy as possible to follow the process and make it easier to follow than to not follow whenever and wherever you can. Some processes need to have some level of complexity to control risk; these risks need to be assessed and controls built into the process, but still try and keep it as simple as possible. Don't overcomplicate it!

What's in a plan?

Planning is a very broad term, we all do it no matter what part of the business we are in. Even when we don't think we are planning, we are still planning. We've all heard the old saying "Failure to plan is planning to fail", one of Benjamin Franklin's many famous quotes. This is truer than you may think.

Anyone who has read any of my books will know just how much of a planner I am. I'm bordering on a psychological planning addiction! Being an ISTJ personality type (and at the extreme in most areas) I plan everything to the details. Even to the point of counting the sausages for a BBQ to ensure I have sufficient inventory to meet demand, without excessive waste! Yes, I know I have a problem... But I do understand not everyone is, can be, or even should be as focussed (or mental) with their planning as me.

But, as we know, "Failure to plan is planning to fail"!! So how do we turn this planning into a process that can be followed? We cannot plan the same way for every project or for every business; it just won't work. We need some knowledge of the business, or of the process to make the planning process the right fit, otherwise if we try and make a planning process that is one size fits all, we will create one of three outcomes:

1) A good fit
2) Waste in the planning process through over planning
3) Insufficient planning to ensure an effective process or

project

So we have a 33% chance of hitting the target! That's simply not good enough.

There are some rules that I believe we can follow that allow us to quickly determine the right level of planning. Now before I get to the rules, I just want to discuss what we plan for. Many people think of planning being for project management. This is correct, however we also plan for sales, supply chain, inventory, manufacturing, administration, shipping etc etc. We plan for every part of our business even if you're in the service or information industries. To make the rules simpler to write down, I am talking generically about planning.

Rule number 1: Before we can apply the rules we need a default. As a team, business, organisation, whatever you want to call yourselves you need to have a default planning methodology and level of detail that is applied. There are many different planning methodologies and even more planning tools that a quick search on Google will bring up (36,900,000 results!). Select, or even better develop a system that suits your business.

Rule number 2: The greater the level of importance, the greater the level of detail. Ask this question: how critical is the success of this project?

Not all projects are created equal and not all outcomes have the same level of importance. If the project you are planning has a higher level of importance then you need to increase the level of detail in your planning from the default. The opposite should be done for projects with a lower level of importance.

Rule number 3: The greater the urgency, the greater the level of detail.

The reason for this rule is simple; the greater the urgency, the more likely there could be shortcuts which result in an increase in risk. By going into more detail you make the process more prescriptive thereby reducing the associated risks.

Rule number 4: The above rules apply to monitoring and reporting also.

What does this mean? Well, if you plan but never monitor progress to the plan or report on the progress you may as well not have planned at all. A plan is only as good as its progress; I don't like hearing "we only report by exception". This doesn't work!

You need to monitor and report on progress regularly and rules 2 and 3 above apply here too. The greater the level of importance the more frequent the monitoring and reporting need be. This is because missing milestones will have a bigger impact on the business with this project than with a less important one. The same goes for urgency. The more urgent or the shorter the timeframe, the more frequent the monitoring and reporting need to be. Don't get caught saying "we're too busy getting it done to monitor"; this will more than likely result in failure. When you are too busy, increase it! There is no rule for frequency, however, for example; if you have 2 years to complete, every 3 months may be sufficient. If you have 6 months to complete, this should be monthly (at least). If you have 1 month, then weekly or twice weekly. If you have 1 day then hourly or more.

Follow these rules and you'll be on your way to succeeding with your planning.

The real cost of inventory

We all know inventory is one of the forms of waste in any business. Whether it be stock sitting between processes, raw materials in the warehouse or finished goods. This is just as valid in a service business where in place of materials you may have other forms of inventory in the same stages of the process. We know all of this; it's nothing new or surprising to most of us. But what about all of the hidden waste that comes about as a result of this inventory; this is harder to measure, monitor and can be invisible to much of the organisation.

1) Cost of storage

The real cost of storage is always more than you may first realise. Not only are you paying for all of the raw materials but you are also paying for all of the value adding to that raw material. This includes labour, more raw materials, consumables, resources (power, gas, water etc). And don't forget you are paying for space to actually store the inventory.

2) Cost of material movement

This is one of the most ignored costs of inventory. Whenever I start working with a new business, one of the first things I do is spend some time (usually at least ½ day to a day) watching the stores to see how big this problem is. In most cases I see them moving inventory around to get to other "more important" inventory; I think the worst

I've seen is a business that spent 2 hours every day moving the same parts for over a month before they realised what they were moving wasn't really needed (only after I told them). At $30 per hour, moving this 1 item equated to $1200.00 labour in that month; I don't know how long this had been going on prior to me seeing it!

3) Cost of rework

To those who have spent any time studying lean this one should not be a new one. Every time you build a piece of inventory you are increasing the likelihood of this waste occurring. When a part goes into inventory it is not uncommon for one of the following to occur: it may get damaged; it will probably get dirty, it may just get "old". In all of these cases, it will require rework, unless you are willing and happy to pass on poor quality; which I hope you're not!

4) Cost of obsoletion

Another hidden or often invisible cost of inventory and depending on your industry and business this may be a big or small cost. In businesses where product changes are frequent (this can be an evolutionary or revolutionary change) this cost will be greater. If yours is a business that maintains inventory at all or most stages of the process then this will be a very great cost. A change to the product will effect: product within the process (this is often the calculated cost of change); inventory in finished goods (again, this is often in the calculated cost of change); all part finished or subassemblies of parts; raw materials in your warehouse; raw materials in transit; raw materials on order or on kanban. The last three are the often forgotten or uncalculated costs that can cause surprises when the changes are finalised and costs rolled up.

5) Opportunity cost
There are two major areas of this hidden cost.

The first is the missed opportunities for the space used to facilitate the storage of the inventory. This calculation should not only include the storage of finished goods and raw materials in the warehouse, but should also include inventory within the process and across the business.

The second is the opportunity costs for all of the resources outlined in the above areas. This is more of a challenge to calculate but is often greater in value than the first. Every time you store, move, clean, rework and reprocess takes your team members away from adding value at that moment. Lean is all about increasing the value add portion and decreasing the non-value add portion of work performed; we sometimes get too engrossed in what we are doing to remember what lean is really about, bring it back to the basics. So this cost is all about how our inventory is taking us further away from our lean objectives.

Change management

Change is a constant (or almost a constant) in any business regardless of the size or type. Not all change is big; it can be a small change that is almost insignificant. This is the best type of change, small regular changes are the backbone of lean and continual improvement philosophies. Small change is a process of its own and doesn't really create the dramatic cultural issues that a medium or large change can bring as a side effect. Today we are discussing some ideas I use to assist in rolling out change to eliminate or at least reduce the impacts the change has on both the organisation and the external stake holders.

I follow a simple 4 step process:

1) Why?
We ask this question for a purpose; change should only be undertaken for a purpose. Change for the sake of change itself is an added waste (which I would categorise under over-processing). We should be able to accurately and succinctly define why we are undertaking the change and what issues, problems or opportunities this change will eliminate or support.

Change as a reaction without proper planning is another form of waste and will not only result in rework of the change process but will also have a negative impact on the morale and culture of the teams and may also result in a reduced customer experience.

Firstly determine why the change is necessary and then define it. Give it some scope.

2) What?
Once we have defined why we are making a change it is necessary to determine what needs to change. Be as specific as possible during this step. I like to follow another lean example and create a current state and future state map. If you already have a library of current state maps to feed into this it's even better as you'll save yourself some time here; but I would still review them to make sure they are accurate and still a relevant guide to the current state. This can be a Value Stream Map, a Process Map, a SIPOC etc. what it is doesn't really matter as long as the details are there.

Then create a future state to show how the business will capture any value adding work from the current state after the changes have occurred. By doing this you will see any processes, actions etc. that may be missed by the changes and ensure your current levels of service are at least maintained; hopefully enhanced!

3) Action
This step should be the easy one, but it's quite often poorly executed. The simplest way to do this right is to

create an action plan with responsibilities and due dates clearly defined so you can measure the actions taken and ensure you achieve the desired outcomes.

The second part of this step is to take the action with gusto! Get it done as fast as possible (by still maintaining quality) to reduce the impact on all involved. A word of caution, too fast is as bad, if not worse than too slow. If you follow the first two steps then too fast shouldn't be a problem as you have planned it properly.

4) Review

I usually undertake a review at 1 month and 3 months of post implementation to check how the changes are going. Check for morale impact, customer impact, financial impacts etc. against the objectives planned and planned outcomes.

The similarity to the PDCA cycle here is not a coincidence; this simple cycle can be used everywhere in every business.

When doing nothing is doing a whole lot

This may come across a little strange to hear someone who usually is an advocate for change saying sometimes doing nothing is the right thing to do. But sometimes, just sometimes doing nothing is what the situation calls for.

We've all known the type of boss, they shoot off requests or tasks without thinking the situation through. If you set to action on every request they make you would quickly run out of time and energy; and before you could complete the first task, 3 new ones have come across your desk, some of which are conflicting with the others. This is not only a trait of some bosses; in every business there are many of these people, and they are not intentionally doing the wrong thing. They are quick thinkers, have many ideas and are only operating in the best interests of the business (in their own mind at least).

What do I do when this personality type crosses my path? After the initial assessment period to learn the people and the boundaries I will ignore many if not most of the requests for a period of time before actioning. I usually wait at least 24 hours, sometimes a week or more, depending on the request and my opinion of its importance. This gives a period of time for the conflicting instruction to come through. I then go and have the conversation with them to clarify which direction we are going. I look at it like a cooling off period for their ideas.

There is an obvious risk to my longevity by following this practice and I don't encourage you do this on your first day in a new job, but I also believe we all have to take some responsibility over those things we can control. We cannot easily control what requests come our way, but we can control how we act and respond to these requests.

Very, very rarely am I caught out by not commencing an action as I only do this with certain people, once I know them. I do however save myself many hours of wasted effort.

My most common 3 answers

I'm often asked my opinion of what someone should do to improve their business. It's a difficult question to answer without knowing their specific business and circumstances. But if were to give my top 3 things that I see businesses doing poorly, that if improved would make a big impact this is what I'd say...

1) Understand and meet the customer's needs

This may seem overly obvious, but you wouldn't believe the number of times I see businesses that have forgotten what it is the customer wants or even why they exist. It's a basic rule, if you don't understand what the customer wants, how can you meet their needs? Now I hear all of the people quoting Henry Ford here saying "If I asked people what they wanted they would have said faster horses". Well this may be true, however it isn't every day we have a real disrupter in our midst; so unless you are a market disrupter, you're better off understanding what the customer needs.

2) Want to know the truth

To succeed you need a desire for what isn't right so you can go about fixing it. Too often I hear people say they want to know the issues so they can be fixed, however when it comes to it, they don't really want to know. I don't know if this desire can be taught or not but this is a real necessity. If you don't have it, find someone who does so they can complement you. This goes beyond just wanting to identify problems in your business unit, it should be spread across the entire business. Be generally truthful in your business dealings and others will be truthful with you.

3) Look after your people

Unless you are a micro company (a solopreneur is the latest name) you need people in your business. Your success is dependent and in some ways is a manifestation of their success and abilities. Good staff are hard to find and even harder to keep. Look after your staff and they will look after you, the more staff you have the more important this is. Another simple, yet overlooked business principle and one we tend to forget when the business gets busier, but mustn't be forgotten.

So there you have it, this isn't every solution to every business problem, however get these right and you'll have a lot less problems to deal with and by contrast, more success.

The good old to do list

I recently read a headline about the death of the To Do List because of the "pressure" the list adds to the list owner. Really? Too much pressure!

I wouldn't normally discuss another bloggers post however this one I felt the need to rebuff. To call for the To Do List to be culled from an entire business, let alone entire businesses is just like calling for all cats to be culled for a single scratch. Simply, if you can't handle the pressure of a job, then get out and do something less stressful.

Rant over...

But I thought I'd share how I use my To Do List. As any regular reader would know, I'm a big planner, however I'm not a religious user of the To Do List. I tend to use a number of different approaches depending on how critical the task is and not surprisingly I use mostly technology for developing and using my lists. For general things I have to do I have to do I use Evernote; I use the checkbox note and have the note linked to my PC, iPhone and iPad to allow synchronised access to the list wherever I am. It is a single list that rolls over to the next day.

For critical, time sensitive tasks I will allocate time in my schedule in Outlook to complete the tasks in-line with the due date. For a time sensitive reminder rather than a task I still utilise Outlook, however in this instance I set a reminder (in the case of an email trigger, I set a reminder against the actual email). Once again, this is all synchronised across all of my devices.

We are in such a technological era for time management it baffles me how anyone would want to not use it. We are so lucky to be working in this era where we are so empowered to manage our own time rather than be managed. Rather than feel stressed by today's "never off" pressures, why not embrace today "always on" opportunities.

Over-Delegation

Is it possible to overdo delegation? For years I have been told I need to delegate more as a leader in business; I know many of you have been told the same thing. We see so many articles on the art of delegation and how to do it best. Well, I'm going to take a different slant on delegation; is it possible to overdo it? Can you delegate too much?

Well I guess it depends on why you are delegating; there are a couple of reasons why you delegate.

1) Delegation to alleviate workload – If this is your primary reason for delegating then you are on the right track. You need to understand what is your core purpose and work on these activities yourself; activities that are not your core should be delegated to allow you more time to work on what it is you do best and what makes you money. However, if you are just starting out and you do not have the customer base to max out your availability then you should probably try and so what you can yourself (If you haven't got the capability, see number 3 below).

2) Delegation to increase team capability – This is an important type of delegation. It's not always just about freeing up your time. Delegating to other team members can be used as a good way to increase the teams overall capability and capacity. This should be done before you <u>need</u> to due to

workload as there will be training involved with this type of delegation.

3) Delegation to tap into higher capability – Similar to the first one, this delegation though is about capability rather than capacity. Unless you want to use it as a learning experience, you should outsource what you're not very good at. Obviously, there is a cost to this if it is true outsourcing. If you have an expert on the subject in your team, then you should really be delegating wherever you can.

4) Delegation for the sake of delegation – I see this a bit unfortunately. Delegation for the sake of delegation is a sign of a much bigger issue. There is nothing more frustrating than seeing a manager of a business not busy because they have delegated all of their work. Yes delegation is important, but if you don't have enough work left for yourself then your team is too big! Don't confuse not having enough work with having some downtime though; these are two totally different things. All leaders and managers should have time allocated for free thinking – this is not doing nothing!

I've realise there's been a bit of a trend in my blogs for the past few weeks; purpose. Believe it or not, this isn't actually intentional but is just a coincidence and I guess a symptom of my current mindset and what I see as important in business at the moment. This one isn't much different; stick to your core purpose and delegate the rest unless, you're not busy enough, you want to train someone, or you want to learn something.

Customer service

I had to take my car in for a scheduled service this morning. I've been out of the automotive game for a few years now and was happily impressed with the swiftness of service and attention to the customer satisfaction. Let's take a look at the dropping off process; there are definite areas that can and should be improved, however the process base is quite high.

1) The book-in process:
   This process was easy, so easy I did it while on my holiday via SMS. I simply sent a text message with my car registration and preferred date. I then received an email and reply text confirming the booking.

2) The drop off:
   This is where it often loses customer focus. Happily this was not the case. Simple easy process; yes, there was quite a queue at the Service Counter, in the 5 minutes I was there 8 customers were served by 3 staff. Preparation was the big key to success here with documentation printed and service jobs raised for every car dropped off before the customer arrived.

3) The pick up:
   Well, this turned out to be the most streamlined part of the entire process. Not only do they want to get the cars in quickly for service, they are intent on getting the customer back into their life after the work is complete.

This was a scheduled service with a couple of warranty items to look into. Firstly I got a phone call when the car was ready for pick up; saved me ringing them to find out. I intentionally arrived a little later than I said I would to see how they would operate under a little pressure. The workshop closed at 5:30; I arrived at 5:28. I walked in and let them know what I was there for; they had the paperwork for the service printed and ready to go in front of me and were running through the completed work within seconds. They then proceeded to take me out to the car to discuss the work carried out for the warranty items. I was in the car and ready to go by 5:32; it helped that no money had to exchange hands.

Overall, a very easy process that left me, as a customer feeling happy, and as a consultant feeling quite impressed. We can all learn from the simplicity of the process.

Now, we all have different businesses and different business types, however we can all learn something from this example. Every step in the process was not only refined to be as efficient for the company to eliminate waste, but the same processes seemed to have the satisfaction of the customer in mind. It can be easy to forget about the customer when we are busy in the details of our jobs; but remember even if the customer isn't always right, they are always important!

Before root cause

How often do you take the time to understand why something you or your team were working towards didn't work out? This is really an investment of time; I say it's an investment because if this is done properly then there will be a return on the investment. Done poorly and there is nothing but lost opportunity.

This is not the place to explain how root cause analysis works or what the process is; today I will be discussing why it works and how not conducting RCA will cost you. These costs are very often overlooked or ignored.

Firstly, let me talk about the different attitudes that may exist in your business; there are only two things worse than a business having errors in its processing. The first is not knowing about the issues; if you don't know you've got a problem, how can you fix it? The second and absolute worst is when a business knows it has an issue and does nothing about it. The first is excusable, you don't know what you don't know, the second is inexcusable.

Identifying the issues or problems (yes, they are problems and opportunities, but let's not sugar coat it) is a process in itself. The big problems will make themselves known by creating big symptoms that cannot go unnoticed, but it is often the smaller problems that bubble away in the background unnoticed that result in job losses and businesses going under; these are the ones we have to go looking for. Long before root cause analysis we have to know what the problem is and we can do this only through the right measurement, monitoring and reporting systems. Ideally these provide the business with accurate timely lead indicators that show up problems before the usual lag indicators would. This gives the business an opportunity to conduct RCA and implement corrective actions before the big symptoms can occur.

Often in business we set our KPI's and other measurement systems and forget them, other than collecting data. Set and forget is not good enough, we need to regularly review both the indicators and the systems to ensure they are relevant and providing us with the right information to make the right decisions. So get to it, review yours!

The 5S System

Nearly every time I go into a business the first lean tool I train and implement is 5S. Why? There are two reasons for this trend.

1) The first reason is obvious. Most businesses have poor housekeeping! Now 5S is much more than housekeeping I know. But the fact remains that many businesses do have poor housekeeping standards or lack of standards. It's a shame that many managers and business owners don't understand what impact this poor housekeeping has on their business. Poor housekeeping will impact safety, quality, delivery, morale and cost. All five of the major performance measures will be negatively impacted by poor housekeeping.

2) The second reason is because 5S is one of the foundations of every other improvement you make to your business. Without a good 5S system in place other improvements you undertake will be difficult to realise and sustain. This is due firstly to the environment a 5S system will create and secondly due to the lessons and culture shift that the implementation of a 5S system will deliver.

Your 60 Minute Lean Business – 5S Implementation Guide is the first of a new series of books designed to take the hassle out of learning the lean tools. Each guide is structured to allow easy understanding and fast implementation.

How do you measure?

Measuring the outputs of a process or service may seem like quite an easy thing to do. Unfortunately many organisations get this wrong. What is the impact of getting this wrong? Read on...

Recently I undertook some consultancy work for a Local Government department. They had a problem delivering a certain service within the regulatory timeframes for many years. They were required to report the performance of this service both to the community through their annual report and also to the State Government. The poor results had been under high scrutiny for many years and many internal reviews and improvement projects had been undertaken. While there had been significant improvements, the outputs remained consistently below the targets (which were quite low).

When I was requested to review the process the first action was to define the problem. Now this seemed quite easy and together with the Manager and Team Leader we put together a problem definition statement along the lines of meeting the KPI targets and quality outputs. On the first day of actually reviewing and challenging what I was seeing, it became quite apparent that the data being used to populate the reports was in fact questionable at best. They had a problem with the data integrity!

I decided to collect some evidence of what I suspected. Over the next two weeks I collected my own data to compare with the official data. Not to my surprise there was significant difference. It turned out that on many occasions the process had in fact met or exceeded the targets. One of the major problems was in fact with the data collection and integrity rather than the process. There were concerns over the process, however without first having a reliable data collection and reporting method it was impossible to measure the impact of any improvements.

There are two morals to this story.

1. Measure the right things in the right way

2. The problem definition should be more than a perceived problem. Challenge your PDS through root cause analysis

Know when to strike

So how do you know when the timing is just right for you to rollout that change you've been planning?

The time is always right! I believe whenever you start is the right time. Sure, some things may need to wait for more finances, the right contacts or even the right stage in the market maturity. But if you wait for those to be right before you start you will miss the boat!

Take the first step now, today. Get off the computer (bookmark this page first!) and get started on that project. Whatever it is, make that first step. Pick up the phone and make that call. Start storyboarding. Whatever the project, there is always something you can do today to make a start.

I'm also a big believer in NOT waiting until it is 100% ready before starting. Many people hide behind the perfectionist tag and never actually achieve their goals because they are working on perfection before sharing. Here's a secret, you will never achieve perfection! Get it out there, share your project with others and get their feedback. Then you can make the necessary changes - continual improvement cannot be achieved unless you start. Follow the Plan, Do, Check, Act cycle and you'll be on your way!

Now, what are you waiting for?

What is a lean business?

It is probably best to first explain what a lean business is not. Most businesses (even some that are seemingly fairly successful) are not operated in a lean way. The term lean can be quite confusing and can give business owners and managers the wrong idea.

Many businesses that attempt to operate in a lean way tend to take the title "Lean" and try to operate their business with lean resources. If this occurs during or after running some lean manufacturing programs or kaizen events then the result will invariably be a halt or even reversal of progress made through the lean initiatives - this is due to the overburden of labour resources. This can be equally detrimental in a manufacturing or office environment.

What does a lean business really look like?

A lean business is one that has or is in the process of identifying the following traits:

Has a well defined strategic / business plan

Has a very clear understanding of its current processes throughout the business

Has a strong understanding of what its customers define "value adding"

Understands how all of its internal processes add value to its customers

Has defined a future state for all internal processes to remove any non-value adding processes

Has identified gaps between the current and future states

Has a clear action plan for all gaps

Has communicated all of the above to internal and external stakeholders

Has resourced the program and resulting action plan

Every one of the above are important for the successful implementation of a sustainable lean program. Obviously not all will be in place from the beginning, however without the last one it will be very difficult to attain most of the others.

So to sum up; obviously to even set the program in motion you will need management with some foresight, understanding and desire to achieve success through the implementation of a lean program. However if asked what is the single most important factor in achieving a successful & sustainable lean business, my answer would be "sufficient resources".

This answer is the opposite of the reality seen in so many businesses. So rather than reducing resources each time an efficiency gain is made (to make sure everyone is working 100

- 110% on their core role) change that mindset so your employees are working 80% on their core role and 20% on further lean initiatives or improvements.

The seven wastes

I'm sure you have heard of the 7 waste of manufacturing.

These are:

Walking

Overproduction

Rework

Motion

overProcessing

Inventory

Transportation

An easy way to remember these is to use the acronym "WORMPIT". There are a couple of different terminologies in use by different practioners, however they all cover the same wastes.

Of all of these wastes, overproduction is the greatest waste. Overproduction contributes to all other wastes. With overproduction, you will also find Inventory, Transportation, Walking, Rework, Motion, and often overprocessing.

Remember, a waste is any action that the customer is not willing to pay for.

What went wrong?

Often I hear people saying they have tried lean before and it didn't work, so why try it again. The simple answer is, if all of the circumstances are the same as last time then you probably shouldn't bother.

Why is this? To answer this let's take a look at some common reasons for a lean program not bringing the desired results.

1. Lack of leadership support

2. Lack of understanding within the leadership group

3. Unclear organisational goals

4. Goals contrasting to lean manufacturing outcomes

When any of these factors are present it will be very difficult to implement a sustainable lean business system.

The most common reason for a lean program to fail in my experience is due to misaligned business goals; particularly expected outcomes from the program. Too often the outcomes desired from a lean program are a reduction in costs. i.e. cost cutting.

When a cost cutting project is portrayed as a lean program the results will not be "lean" at all. This is because cost cutting is a very short term view for any organisation, whereas a lean business system is a long term sustainable business plan.

The irony is that in every instance, a well developed and implemented lean business system will provide a reduction in costs and an increase in profits. By focussing on the outcomes for the customer; eliminating waste, built in quality, safety and respecting employees; the cost reductions will become almost automatic.

Does the name really matter?

What is a kaizen event? I've just sat through 3 hours of a "kaizen event" and it got me thinking about the term and how every business uses it differently. I know this will strike a nerve with some hard core TPS folks out there, but does it really matter how the term is used?

Surely all that matters is the results achieved and realized through the process of reviewing and analysing your processes. I see a lot of forums and posts on the internet where experts are complaining about the incorrect use of lean / TPS / Six Sigma terminology and it's my belief that this stubborn focus (hang up) on the terminology and process is not only holding back lean but is in fact suffocating the take up of effective improvement.

This may seem strange that a process guy is challenging the stubborn "must follow the process of kaizen" mentality but as with any process, it must work. You cannot take a manufacturing process from one company and expect it to work exactly the same in a company in a different segment, in a different country. There are so many reasons why the process needs to be 'personalized' to fit the business needs and culture. Culture plays a big part in improvement. It is almost disrespectful to the people to expect them to take on a process without having input into it and quite contradictory to the TPS methods. Kaizen itself means to make change with the involvement of everyone, by imposing a process to this goes against the whole philosophy...

Now what is important is the results you and your business achieve through the use of whatever tools you find help you. We all have our favourite set of tools that we rely heavily on but it is important as facilitators, mentors etc. that we are flexible enough in our approach to ensure our customers (process owners) buy-in and improve - that's how we measure our success, not in the use of words or tools.

Just some food for thought...

The importance of contingencies

As I write this I am sitting in the Qantas Lounge at Perth Domestic Airport. Ordinarily I try to get to the airport a good hour before necessary as I don't like to rush around. Today I completed my work early and decided to sit at the airport and wait for my flight home rather than wait at work. I'm not sure why, it just seemed a good idea.

Well when I arrived at the airport I entered the Qantas Terminal and noticed something I hadn't seen for quite a while. Not since they commissioned the automatic Baggage Drop-off systems so prevalent at airports around the world. Well today they were all broken; we had unplanned downtime! And because the failure was in the system side, every station went down. Now I have to commend Qantas here for how they handled it. There were long queues around the terminal, however they do have a couple of pods that are usually closed but today were open. The queues did move reasonably fast. I'm sure everyone made their flights and a bad situation was recovered through good planning and the presence of contingency methods.

This unplanned downtime incident reminded how important it is for businesses to have planned contingency methods for when the downtime occurs. No matter how effective your TPM is, there will be circumstances that result in unplanned downtime at some point in your business journey.

Have a look at your business, how much do you depend on certain plant? Or even worse, how much does the business rely on certain individuals? For every piece of critical plant and every significant role in the business you should have a contingency plan. This can be as simple as temporarily outsourcing or job sharing. For very significant or costly processes it may be a backup piece of plant. What the solution is isn't the most important thing. What is important is business continuity.

Effectiveness

Anyone who knows me knows I am a lean junkie! I live and breathe lean, in both my professional and person lives. I use lean principles every day in my work, both for my own activities and more obviously when I'm training and facilitating as a lean business coach. But I also use lean principles in my everyday life at home. Whether it is making breakfast, shaving, cooking or washing the car, I am always looking for ways to be more efficient.

Today I washed my car and mowed my lawn; while doing the latter I came to think to myself "what if people at work could see how I'm mowing my lawn, how would I be able to explain my process?" You see, there are two things that I am anal about, one is washing my car, the second and most anal is how I maintain my lawn. I have a three mow cycle that I follow; mow 1, I mow the lawn clockwise in a circular motion; mow 2, I mow the lawn counter-clockwise in a circular motion; mow 3, I mow the lawn longitudinally, followed by laterally. Yes that's right, on mow 3 I mow the lawn twice in two different directions!

How can this lean junkie, apparently waste time by mowing the lawn in this inefficient manner? Well, efficiency is only one part of being lean. Before you can even measure efficiency, you have to determine what the standard is. Effectiveness is the ability to achieve the standard (or purpose). I have a high standard for my lawn mowing, the process outlined above is the most efficient way of achieving and maintaining that standard. It would probably be more efficient for me to outsource the process, however another part of the purpose is enjoyment (yes I am strange, I enjoy cutting my lawn!).

In your business, when deploying lean don't forget about setting the standards. Efficiency without effectiveness is a failed deployment.

Player or Spectator?

Which one are you? If I were to ask your peers, would they agree with your answer? The answer to these two simple questions can tell a whole lot about your success. There is no sitting on the fence here, it has to be one or the other and you can choose which direction you take.

A spectator does sit on the fence, they sit in the grandstand and watch as things unfold; no matter what area of their life, they let it be as it will. A spectator will go along with the decisions of others, they will not "rock the boat" and float through life at the mercy of the currents. Where they end up is determined by others and their actions. Spectators don't like making decisions for themselves or for others, they are the followers who love a democracy or even better a dictatorship (as long as they are being dictated). Spectators are quite often also the complainers; complaining when things don't go their way or they didn't get that pay rise even though they aren't willing to go after what they want.

On the other hand, a player takes their destiny into their own hands and makes things happen. Players are decision makers who thrive on the opportunity to make a difference to a project, a business, a life. They see a vision, work out a plan (or follow a plan) and work towards getting the results; when something gets in their way they work out a new plan. They don't just go to their boss or their friends and complain about the outcome, they make the outcome.

Not only do you NOW have to go and assess whether you are a player or a spectator; you have to decide which you want to be? Because not everyone wants to be a player. It is also a good idea to understand those you work with regularly to understand if they are players or spectators; this is especially important if you are a leader of others – you should know the make-up of your team.

www.ingramcontent.com/pod-product-compliance
Lightning Source LLC
Chambersburg PA
CBHW070321190526
45169CB00005B/1693